SUMMARY OF

THE REAL ANTHONY FAUCI

Bill Gates, Big Pharma and the Global War on Democracy and Public Health

BY ROBERT F. KENNEDY JR

JONATHAN COVEY

All rights reserved, No part of this publication may be reproduced or distributed in any form or by any means, without the prior written permission of the publisher, except in the case of brief quotations embodied in critical reviews and certain other noncommercial uses permitted by copyright law.

Copyright©2021 by JONATHAN COVEY.

INTRODUCTION

CHAPTER ONE

REVIEW OF THE BOOK

INTRODUCTION

Fauci uses freely available resources to hospitals, universities, and magazines, and exerts extraordinary influence on thousands of influential doctors and scientists.

These are the same doctors who appear on network news broadcasts, post on influential media sites, and create and defend the official story of drug cartels.

Fauci rarely fulfills NIAID's traditional mission of studying the causes of the epidemic of allergic and autoimmune diseases. In the 1960s, today it is 54% when obesity is taken into account.

Instead of fighting the rise in chronic disease, Forch transforms NIAID from a world-class regulatory agency into a product incubator for major pharmaceutical companies, with new drugs and vaccines and patents often shared by him, his agents, and his staff. And often share loyalty.

CHAPTER ONE

REVIEW OF THE BOOK

Fauci and his four handpicked alternatives will participate in a multi-million dollar loyalty from the sale of Moderna's COVID vaccine, co-developed by Moderna and NIAID.

Fauci has become a major supporter of government prisoners of war, a weakening of democracy, and public health by the pharmaceutical industry.

Genuine Anthony Fauci reveals, Fauci has steadily failed upwards. His legacy is that he continues to use medicines; pays prescription drugs almost three times as much as people in dozens of other countries, is in poor health, and has a larger population than other wealthy countries.

Today, prescription drugs, often developed by the National Institutes of Health (NIH) while the National Institutes of Health (NIH) was enrolled in NIAID at NIH, are the third leading cause of death in the United States.

This book also shows how Fauci and his pharmaceutical cohort benefit from illness, but not much from health.

Fauci survived half a century in his government post-he is J. Edgar Hoover in Public Health-By succumbing and profiting to the interests of pharmaceuticals.

He started his career in collaboration with pharmaceutical companies early in the AIDS crisis to thwart safe and effective non-patent treatment for AIDS.

Fauci coordinated fraudulent research and pressured US Food and Drug Administration (FDA) regulators to approve a deadly chemotherapy regimen that he knew was worthless to AIDS. The FDA has discovered that AZT is too toxic for human use. Many researchers today claim that AZT killed far more people than AIDS. The corrupt intervention of

Fauci has made AZT the most expensive over-the-counter drug in history, at $ 10,000 per patient per year. This is a multi-billion dollar drug on GlaxoSmithKline.

Fauci repeatedly violated federal law allowing his pharmaceutical partners to use poor, dark-skinned children as experimental rats in deadly experiments with toxic AIDS and cancer chemotherapy.

In 2005, Congress cited the agency for consistently breaking federal law in lawless experiments involving

Black and Hispanic orphans in nursing homes in New York and six other states.

A long list of unethical and slaughtered experiments on Africans has caused havoc and tragedy throughout the continent, especially between children and pregnant mothers. Each vaccine funded by

Fauci and Bill Gates (polio, DPT, malaria, meningitis, tetanus, HIV) could have caused far more injuries and deaths than prevented worldwide.

In early 2000, Fauci Gates shook hands at Gates' $ 147 million mansion library in Seattle, with endless growth potential, an increasingly profitable $ 60 billion global. We have established a partnership aimed at managing a successful vaccine company.

In 2009, Gates stood before the United Nations declared "a decade of vaccines." He provided the US $ 10 billion to build regulatory, political, media, and inpatient infrastructure with the goal of immunizing the global population with multiple vaccinations by 2020.

The PharmaFauciGates Alliance manages its global health policy through a means of financing and carefully nurturing personal relationships with heads of state, major media, and social media institutions.

Gates and Forch are now with widespread influence to stall the world economy, abolish civil and constitutional rights, carry out police surveillance, and create the greatest global wealth surge in human history. We are exercising unprecedented power.

This book reveals how Fauci, Gates, and their collaborators work together.

• Invented, armed, and sold novels of fraudulently manufactured pandemic parades such as bird flu (2005), swine flu (2009), and deer (2015-2016). Vaccine their pharmaceutical partners to empower engineers in public health and aides to Gates' international organizations.

• Using gain of function experiments, in Wuhan and other locations in China, in an unstable and poorly regulated laboratory, working with the Chinese Pentagon, of weapon-grade microorganisms. Pandemic super bacteria were grown under conditions that almost certainly ensured escape. Grab the army and the conspiracy to sow biological weapons.

• Made a series of forecasts for the imminent COVID 19 pandemic-almost to this day. Their precise fortune-telling treats Gates and Forch as religious gods, protects them from public criticism, and denounces their

allegations as heretics and "conspirators," rough, deceptive, and scientific. Further threatened the illiterate media. The prestigious mainstream media upheld Fauci's plan to conceal the origin of COVID at the Wuhan Institute.

• Worked with US, European, and Chinese government technocrats, military and intelligence planners, and health authorities to stage sophisticated pandemic simulations and reproductive games. Such exercises, sponsored by the Global Reserve Oversight Committee, aim to implement global totalitarianism, including compulsory masking, bans, mass promotion, and censorship, with the ultimate goal of ordering forced vaccination of 7 billion people. Lay the foundation for. ?

• Practice psychological warfare techniques in each simulation to cause confusion, stir fear, destroy the economy, destroy public morals, and curb individual self-expression, then self-government was carried out.

COVID19 Pandemic

Fanning Fearial Anthony Fauci manages how Fauci, Gates, and their cohorts manage media, scientific journals, major government and territorial agencies, influential scientists, and physicians. Relentlessly censors

Publicity, muzzle discussions, and dissenting opinions about the pathogenicity and etiology of COVID 19, explaining what has made the public a more disturbing flood.

Gates and Fauci contacted each other almost daily during the blockade and coordinated virtually all decisions regarding COVID 19 measures with each other.

They effectively put people around the world under house arrest and flooded mainstream and social media with propaganda aimed at terrorism.

To justify the implementation of strict measures, Gates and Forch systematically fueled irrational fear, suppressed common sense, and induced a type of mass psychosis known as "Stockholm Syndrome."

They are the only safe escape from prisoners of war, with gratitude to the prisoners of war and full and unconditional obedience to the experimental, poorly tested, accelerated, irresponsible COVID vaccine. Inspired by the belief that "returns to normal" As the pandemic progressed, Gates and Forch advocated: ▪

- Rogue models and algorithms that deliberately exaggerate COVID 19 loss forecasts to streamline tight blockades.

- Intentionally increasing the number of

COVID cases by approximately 90% through anointed and fraudulent PCR tests.

- Coroners promoted the adoption of new unprecedented instructions for fraudulently indicating COVID as a cause of death. Result COVID 19-Test.

- Hydroxychloroquine and many other drugs that could have quickly ended a pandemic and saved hundreds of thousands of lives have discredited all early COVID 19 treatments.

As expected, Fauci's policies during the COVID crisis resulted in the United States accounting for 20% of the world's COVID deaths, even though it accounted for only 4.2% of the world's population. This is another example of Fauci's failure to stop.

As this book reveals, Fauci's COVID policy also creates new insidious authoritarianism, driving America into a slippery descent towards a dark future as a dark totalitarian security and surveillance nation.

Made in the USA
Las Vegas, NV
29 August 2022